Snakes

Sonia Hernandez-Divers

ISBN 978-0-431125-61-8 (hardback)

ISBN 978-0-431125-61-8 (paperback)

British Library Cataloguing in Publication Data

Raintree

www.raintreepublishers.co.uk

Visit our website to find out more information about Raintree books.

To order:

☎ Phone 0845 6044371
📠 Fax +44 (0) 1865 312263
💻 Email myorders@capstonepub.co.uk

Customers from outside the UK please telephone +44 1865 312262

Edited by Louise Galpine, Megan Cotugno, and Laura Knowles
Designed by Kim Miracle and Ryan Frieson
Picture research by Mica Brancic
Originated by Capstone Global Library Ltd 2010
Printed and bound in China by Leo Paper Products Ltd

Acknowledgements
We would like to thank the following for permission to reproduce photographs: Alamy p. **23 top**; Ardea pp. **28 bottom** (Douglas Napier), **10 top** (Geoff Trinder), **19**; © Capstone Global Library Ltd pp. **41 bottom** (Maria Joannou), **45** (Trevor Clifford), **8, 12 top, 13, 14, 15 top, 15 bottom, 18, 21 top, 21 bottom, 22 top, 22 bottom, 28 top, 29, 30, 31 bottom, 31 top, 33, 34 bottom, 35, 36 top, 36 bottom, 37 top, 38 top, 38 bottom, 39, 41 top, 43 all** (Tudor Photography); © Capstone Publishers pp. **20, 23 bottom, 24 top, 25, 26, 27, 32, 34 top, 37 bottom, 40, 42, 44** (Karon Dubke); Corbis p. **12 bottom**; Heather Angel p. **6**; iStockphoto p. **4** (© Serdar Yagci); Natural Visions p. **9 top** (Brian Rogers); NHPA pp. **9 bottom, 11 top** (Daniel Heuclin), **11 bottom** (James Carmichael Jr), **5 top** (Martin Wendler); OSF pp. **7 top** (www.photolibrary.com/David M Dennis), **16** (www.photolibrary.com/Mike Price); Photolibrary pp. **17 top, 17 bottom**; Science Photo Library pp. **5 bottom** (Tom McHugh), **10 bottom**; Shutterstock p. **7 bottom**.

Cover photograph of a Trans-Pecos Ratsnake (*Bogertophis subocularis*) reproduced with permission of Getty Images (Dorling Kindersley/© Laura Wickenden).

We would like to thank Judy Tuma and Rob Lee for their invaluable help in the preparation of this book.

Every effort has been made to contact copyright holders of material reproduced in this book. Any omissions will be rectified in subsequent printings if notice is given to the publishers.

Disclaimer
All the Internet addresses (URLs) given in this book were valid at the time of going to press. However, due to the dynamic nature of the Internet, some addresses may have changed, or sites may have changed or ceased to exist since publication. While the author and Publishers regret any inconvenience this may cause readers, no responsibility for any such changes can be accepted by either the author or the Publishers.

No animals were harmed during the process of taking photographs for this series.

Contents

Any words appearing in the text in bold, **like this**, are explained in the glossary.

What is a snake?

Snakes belong to the **reptile** family. Reptiles have no hair and their bodies are covered with scales. They do not make milk for their young and they are **cold-blooded**, which means they need to soak up heat from their surroundings. Other types of reptiles are lizards, turtles, alligators, and crocodiles.

Snakes are long, legless creatures that slither along the ground. They do not have eyelids or external ears. They **shed** all their skin in one piece at regular intervals.

Squeezing to death

Some snakes kill their **prey** by squeezing it. This is called **constriction**. They grab an animal firmly and then wrap their muscular bodies around it, squeezing the animal so it cannot breathe. Eventually, the animal **suffocates**. Once the animal is dead, the snake swallows it whole.

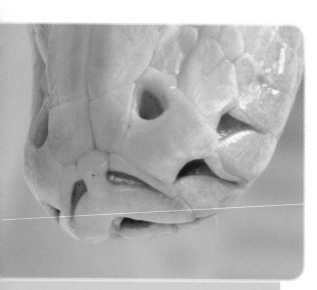

Some snakes have small pits above their lips. These pits are actually heat-sensing organs that allow the snake to sense warm-blooded prey.

DID YOU KNOW?

- All snakes are **carnivorous**, which means they eat other animals.

- Snakes eat large amounts of food at once, and one large meal can take them weeks to digest!

- Some snakes eat fish, while others eat insects, birds, other snakes, eggs, or **rodents**.

- Some **species** of snake can unhinge their jaws so that they can swallow very large animals.

Beware of poison!

About one third of the world's snakes are **venomous**. Venomous snakes have hollow **fangs** on their upper jaw and **venom glands** – small **organs** at the base of the fangs – that make a powerful poison. When the snake bites its prey, **venom** is injected into it. The snake simply waits for the venom to work, before swallowing the dead animal.

This is a type of snake called an anaconda. Anacondas kill their prey by wrapping themselves around the animal and squeezing it tightly until it can no longer breathe.

NEED TO KNOW

- ✪ Snakes are protected by law – which means you are not allowed to catch snakes from the wild.

- ✪ Children are not allowed to buy pets themselves. You should have an adult with you when you buy your pet.

- ✪ Most countries have laws that say that pets must be treated with respect. It is your responsibility to make sure that your snake is healthy and well cared for. Always take your pet to the vet if it is ill or injured.

The fangs of some venomous snakes are so long that they are normally folded back inside their mouth. When the snake strikes to bite, the fangs unfold. The snake bites its prey with the fangs and injects venom into it.

Snake facts

It is useful to know how snakes live and hunt in the wild, because this will help you to understand your own pet snake.

Environmental threat?

Snakes are found in most parts of the world, in a range of different **habitats**. Some **species** of snakes have been introduced in areas to which they are not native. This has caused great damage to the wildlife of those areas. For example, the brown tree snake was introduced to islands in the Pacific Ocean. The snakes thrived on the **prey** available there. Now these snakes are considered pests. They have severely reduced the populations of native birds, small mammals, and even domestic **poultry**.

Grass snakes are common in the United Kingdom. If you are lucky, you might get a glimpse of one **basking** in the sunshine!

DID YOU KNOW?

There are around 3,000 species of snakes in the world. Like most **reptiles**, they live in the warmer parts of our planet. But snakes can be found in a variety of habitats. The bamboo viper lives in the bamboo thickets of China, the dwarf adder lives in the dry, powdery sand deserts of south-west Africa, and the yellow-bellied sea snake spends most of its life floating in the currents of the Indian and Pacific Oceans.

Snakes under threat

Many snake habitats are being threatened. One of the biggest threats is **deforestation**. When forests are cut down, many species lose their homes, **environment**, and food sources. Without the things they require, snakes can no longer survive. In fact, for some snake species, everything needed for their survival completely disappears.

Forest fires and grassland fires not only destroy the snakes' habitats, they can destroy the snakes too. The continued spread of housing and the development of new communities also contribute to the destruction of snakes' habitats. Many snakes also become victims of cars and lorries as they attempt to cross roads. Even the establishment of new farmland can be dangerous - it not only eliminates the native habitats of some snakes, but also spreads **pesticides** which protect the crops but harm the wildlife.

Garter snakes like this one are very common in the USA and can even be found in towns and cities, where they hunt for small insects and fish.

Forest fires kill snakes and other animals, and can ruin their habitat for many years.

Tasting the air

Snakes have a very good sense of smell, but they do not have noses like we do. A snake flicks out its tongue and picks up little invisible **particles** that are floating in the air. When it brings its tongue back into its mouth, it presses it against a special **organ** on the roof of its mouth (called the vomeronasal organ) that detects the "smell" of the particles that the tongue has picked up! So, you could say that a snake "tastes" the air in order to smell it!

Hearing and feeling

Snakes do not have external ears, but because they can feel vibrations they are not completely deaf. For example, if you walk next to a snake, the vibrations that your feet make on the ground are enough for a snake to "hear" you coming.

Even though its scales seem thick, a snake's skin is very sensitive. Snakes can sense very slight temperature changes through their skin. They can also feel when they brush against even the softest things.

This snake is picking up particles from the air on its tongue. In order to "smell" the air, it needs to press the ends of its forked tongue against a special organ on the roof of its mouth.

Snakes' eyes

Most snakes do not have very good eyesight. In fact, you can probably see better than most snakes! They also do not have eyelids. Instead, they have clear scales that cover their eyes. These scales keep their eyes moist and protect them.

Unlike many snakes, blue racers use their eyes to help them find their prey. They travel through grass with their heads above the blades looking out for animals.

SNAKE SOUNDS

Most of the time, snakes are silent, but they can make some interesting noises.

- ✪ Snakes hiss when they are frightened or angry. They do this by forcing air out through their nostrils very fast.

- ✪ Some snakes have a "rattle" on their tail. It is made of segments that bump each other when the snake vibrates its tail. This bumping makes the rattling sound.

The rattlesnake shakes its rattle to warn **predators** to keep away.

Hiding and running

Snakes have a lot of enemies. Hawks, owls, fish, foxes, skunks, raccoons, badgers, and many other animals all eat snakes. So a snake has to be very careful not to be seen or captured.

Most snakes use their colouring as **camouflage** to help them hide. The pattern on a snake's skin usually matches the background of the place where it lives. When a predator approaches, most snakes choose to stay still and blend in with their surroundings until the danger has passed.

Snakes have many enemies in the wild, so they have to stay well hidden or fight back fiercely.

If they are discovered, snakes have to get away! A wild snake that hears a strange noise or sees a large animal approaching will slither away fast. That is why if you go walking in the countryside, all you will probably ever see of a snake is a flash of movement!

Some snakes are incredibly well camouflaged. Can you find the snake in this picture?

FIGHTING BACK

Snakes will defend themselves in several different ways if they are grabbed by a predator:

- ✪ Some snakes have **scent glands** that produce a foul smell. This is meant to convince the predator that the snake would not make a suitable meal!

- ✪ Some snakes try to squeeze the animal that grabs them, by wrapping their bodies around a leg, for example.

- ✪ Some snakes bite, using their sharp, needle-like teeth. Most small snakes only make little pinprick holes when they bite, but large snakes, such as pythons, can strike with force and cause severe wounds.

- ✪ Some snakes are **venomous** and sink their **fangs** into their attackers and inject them with poison. This is very painful and the **venom** of some snakes can kill even quite large animals.

Many venomous snakes use their colouring to scare off predators. For example, the coral snake, which is highly poisonous, has very noticeable coloured bands on its body. These warn predators to stay away. Other snakes have colours similar to venomous snakes, even though they are not poisonous at all. This type of self defence is called mimicking.

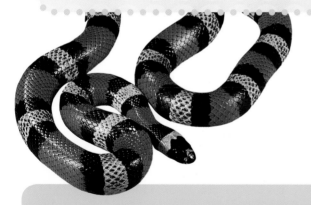

The venomous coral snake (below) has bands of bright colours that warn predators to stay away.

Milk snakes (above) are not venomous but some of them have the same bands of colours as the venomous coral snake. That way predators *think* they are poisonous and avoid eating them.

Is a snake for you?

Some **species** of snakes can make interesting and fun pets, but before you buy one, you should think about some of the plus and minus points of keeping snakes.

The right snake

Only a few species of snake make truly good pets. Others, such as pythons, should not be handled unless you have an experienced adult with you. An adult should always be present when younger children are handling any type of snake. Some snakes – especially poisonous ones – are very dangerous and should not be kept in **captivity**, except by professional snake owners and zoos.

The ideal pet snake should not be poisonous and should not get too big for its owner to handle. Some snakes, such as boa constrictors, can grow up to 3 metres (10 feet) long and need several people to handle them.

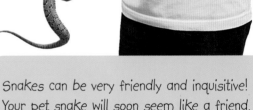

Snakes can be very friendly and inquisitive! Your pet snake will soon seem like a friend.

As well as growing very large, pythons tend to be moody and can strike out and bite their owners. They are not good pets for beginners!

GOOD POINTS

- Snakes are beautiful.
- Many snakes are gentle.
- They are very quiet pets.
- They are easy to keep clean.
- They do not have to be fed very often.
- They are fascinating to watch.

NOT-SO-GOOD POINTS

- Snakes need to be kept warm and dry.
- You will need to buy some special equipment.
- Snakes have to be fed live or frozen rats or mice.
- Snakes can escape easily, and hide anywhere.
- Some species can bite very hard.
- Some snakes are poisonous, and must not be kept as pets.

Yes or no?

If you and your family decide you are ready to keep a snake, great! But remember, being responsible for a living thing can be a lot of work. Most snakes tend to be long-lived – even a small corn snake will live for ten years – so you will be looking after your pet for a long time. Snakes need special care to stay healthy and happy. You will need to do some homework to understand the needs of your pet.

Snakes feed on live or dead mice or rats, which can put some people off keeping snakes as pets.

Choosing your snake

Snakes that have been born in **captivity** are good pets. Never capture a wild snake, or get a wild snake from any source.

There are many different types of snake available from pet shops or snake **breeders**. If you have never owned a pet snake before, it is best to start with a snake that is small, gentle, and easy to look after. Two good examples are the corn snake and the garter snake.

This is a typical corn snake. It has an arrowhead pattern on the top of its head and a golden coloured body with reddish-brown markings.

Corn snakes

Wild corn snakes live in the eastern part of the USA. They live in pine forests, on rocky hillsides, and in farming areas. Corn snakes are most active at night or in the early morning and late evening. They are mainly ground-dwellers, which means it is rare to find them in trees.

Young corn snakes eat small lizards, little frogs, or insects, such as crickets. As they get bigger, they hunt larger animals, such as **rodents**.

DID YOU KNOW?

The scientific name for a corn snake is *Elaphe guttata*. The first word is Latin for "deerskin", because these snakes have soft skin that feels like the hide of a deer. The second word means speckled or spotted, and refers to the markings on their body.

Corn snake colours

Wild corn snakes are covered in red or brown blotches, but in captivity corn snakes have been **bred** to be lots of different colours. You might find one that is completely white, or mostly red, or one that has a wide variety of patterns!

GREAT PETS!

Corn snakes make great pets because:

- ✪ They are not expensive.
- ✪ They do not get very big. They only grow to around 1 metre (3 feet) long.
- ✪ They can live for 15 to 20 years.
- ✪ They are gentle.
- ✪ They are not fussy eaters.
- ✪ They do not have many special needs.

The biggest problem with corn snakes is that they are real escape artists! Once they have got out of their tanks, they can easily hide!

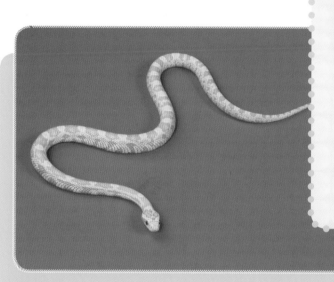

Reptile breeders have bred many different colours of corn snakes. This **albino** corn snake is very pale, with ruby red eyes.

The pattern on this corn snake's belly looks like piano keys!

Rat snakes

How do you think the rat snake got its name? Correct! It eats rats. In the wild, rat snakes eat rats, mice, voles, squirrels, and birds. Young rat snakes eat frogs, lizards, and young mice.

Rat snakes originally come from the USA. They usually live in heavily wooded areas. They have also become used to living around people, so they can often be found in barns or in gardens too. They also spend a lot of time in trees. In most areas of the USA, it is **illegal** to collect wild rat snakes or hurt them in any way because they are **endangered**. The most common rat snake is the black rat snake.

In the wild, rat snakes can have a varied diet of rats, mice, voles, squirrels, and birds.

Noisy tail

The black rat snake has some special scales on its tail that make a rattle-like sound to scare off **predators**. It deliberately imitates rattlesnakes so other animals will leave it alone. But it is not related to rattlesnakes and is not **venomous**.

DID YOU KNOW?

The scientific name for a rat snake is *Elaphe obsoleta*. It shares its first name with the corn snake and they are, in fact, related. Indeed, they are cousins! Some people call corn snakes the red rat snake.

Garter snake colours

Garter snakes all have one, two, or three narrow stripes that run down the entire length of their body. These stripes can be yellow, white, or red. In between the rows of stripes are dark, rather blotchy spots.

The pattern on this garter snake is very clear. Can you count how many stripes the snake has on its body?

A garter snake will usually stretch out when it is held.

GARTER SNAKE FACTS

✪ Garter snakes are usually less than 60 centimetres (24 inches) long.

✪ They are active during the day.

✪ They eat earthworms, insects, and pinkie (newborn) mice.

✪ With proper care, they can live up to six years.

Buying your pet snake

Corn snakes and garter snakes should always be bought from a pet shop or a reptile breeder. Reptile breeders often advertise in newspapers, on the Internet, and in reptile magazines.

Reptile breeders keep and breed reptiles such as snakes and lizards. They can be very helpful because they have lots of experience of looking after snakes. A reptile breeder can give you information on how to care for your snake, where to get snake food, what equipment you will need, and how to keep your snake healthy. A reptile breeder will also show you how to check your snake for common problems.

An **alert** corn snake will flick its tongue often and move around the tank.

TOP TIPS

A good reptile breeder will help you choose which snake is best for you.

✪ You will probably want a snake that looks beautiful, but remember to check that it is also alert and active.

✪ Look at its skin and scales – they should look bright and shiny.

✪ Ideally, you should buy a young snake, so it can get used to you from an early age.

Important questions

Before you buy a pet, you will need to know some basic details about your snake and how to take care of it. Here are some questions to ask the reptile breeder or pet shop owner:

- ✪ Was the snake bred in captivity? You should not buy snakes that have been taken from the wild.

- ✪ How old is it? It is best to buy a young snake.

- ✪ What is it eating? You will need to buy the same food.

- ✪ How often is it eating? This will help you plan meals.

- ✪ How much is the snake eating at one time? This will help you decide how much to feed it.

- ✪ How often is it **shedding** its skin? You will want to make sure that your snake is shedding regularly (see page 38).

WARNING SIGNS

Do not buy a snake that:

- ✪ seems sleepy or is not very active when you hold it

- ✪ is not flicking its tongue

- ✪ has cuts or scrapes on its body

- ✪ has dull skin

- ✪ has **mites** or **ticks** on its body.

This snake has ticks clinging on to its head, between its scales.

What do I need?

Your new pet will need a comfortable place to live. Corn snakes and garter snakes can be kept in tanks, like the ones used for fish. When your snake is young and small, a 20- or 40-litre (4.5- or 9-gallon) tank will be big enough. As time passes, your snake will grow and need a bigger tank. An 80- to 100-litre (18- to 22-gallon) tank will be a good size. Make sure the tank has a secure top made of screening material with small holes. A wood enclosure should have air vents placed on opposite sides, one near the top and the other near the bottom, so that there is good air flow.

KEEP IT IN!

Your snake will spend a great deal of time and effort trying to get out of its tank, so your tank will need a tight-fitting lid! Make sure your tank has a lid that snaps closed or a sliding door that has a lock on it. Never underestimate the strength of your snake. Snakes are bundles of muscle and will push the lids open if they do not fit very tightly!

The tank should be at least as long as your snake, but ideally twice as long. It should also be wide enough for your snake to turn around comfortably.

SUBSTRATE

Substrate is the material you will put on the bottom of the tank. It will give your snake something soft and warm to lie on.

- ✪ Natural materials like topsoil can be used, but they are difficult to keep clean.

- ✪ Pine wood shavings make good substrate because it is easy to remove any soiled shavings.

- ✪ You can also use paper towels, newspaper, or artificial grass for your substrate. They do not look as attractive as wood shavings and will not feel as natural to your snake, but they are very easy to replace. Artificial grass will have to be washed and thoroughly dried before being put back in the tank.

You can cover the bottom of your snake's tank with shavings or torn-up paper towels. It is best to put your snake in a container without shavings when you feed it. That way, the **prey** will not get covered in little pieces of shavings.

Water bowl

Choose a water bowl that is heavy enough to stop your snake from tipping it over. Black rat snakes like to soak in their bowls, so the bowl should also be big and deep enough for them to climb into it.

SAFETY FIRST!

Never use cedar wood shavings as substrate. The fumes from this type of wood can be harmful to your snake.

Make sure you clean the water bowl every day and whenever your snake uses the bowl as a toilet.

21

Shelter

It is very important to give your snake a place to rest! Your pet will like a little plastic house that you can make yourself, or a pile of natural items such as branches or a large, curved piece of bark. You should give your pet a shelter in both the warm and the cooler areas of its tank (see page 27 to find out about tank temperatures).

Cage furniture

Putting rocks and branches in your pet's tank will imitate the snake's **environment** in the wild. Remember, snakes spend a lot of time climbing on and in between rocks and fallen logs to search for their prey. You can put a branch inside the tank so your snake can climb on to it. More importantly, snakes need a hard object, such as a rock, to rub against and get rid of their old skin.

Making a home for your snake is an easy project. Cut a small hole in the side of a medium-sized plastic tub. Make sure there are no sharp edges on the tub. Put it upside down and you have a snake house!

This corn snake has just **shed** its skin. When your snake has completely shed its old skin, remove the shed skin from the tank.

You could also try adding some plastic plants to the tank to make your snake feel more at home. If you want to use real plants, ask a **breeder** to recommend plants and soils that are safe for your pet.

Plastic plants can look attractive and are easy to clean.

All change!

Every once in a while, change all the furniture in your snake's home. This will not confuse your snake – it will just make it feel as if it has moved to a new place! You will notice your snake will flick its tongue and try to re-explore its "new" home. This is good exercise for your pet and will keep it from getting bored.

Adding new items to your snake's home will keep your snake happy.

Looking after your snake

Looking after a snake is a big responsibility. There are lots of things you will need to do on a regular basis.

Keeping things clean

Your snake's tank will need to be cleaned thoroughly every two weeks. Keeping your snake's home clean is the best way to make sure it stays healthy and happy!

Take all the contents out of the tank and clean them individually. The tank can be cleaned with a **reptile**-safe cleaner bought from a pet shop. After using the cleaner, rinse the tank thoroughly with lots of water and then let it dry completely before you put back any of its contents or your snake.

Keep your snake in a separate container while you clean its tank. It can watch you from a safe spot!

TOP TIP

It is a good idea to have a small, plastic container with holes in it where you can put your snake while you clean its home. That way it will not escape and you will not hurt it with any cleaning materials you are using.

When cleaning the tank, you must make sure that the disinfectant you use is not harmful to snakes.

WHEN TO CLEAN

- Every day, change the water in your snake's water bowl so that the water is always fresh.

- Every two days, remove any **faeces** or soiled **substrate** from the tank.

- Every two weeks, clean the entire tank and all its contents.

Home from home

Try to create a home that is as close as possible to that which your snake would experience in the wild. In the wild, a snake would wake up and go to a sunny spot to absorb heat through its skin – this is called **basking**. When it had absorbed enough heat, it would begin to be active and move about. If it got too hot, it would move to a shady area or slither inside a burrow to cool down.

Under-tank heating pads are the best method of heating your tank. They do not give out any light and your snake will not get burned.

Your snake will want to do the same things in its tank. You will need to set up a **heat source** at one end of your snake's tank so that your pet has one very warm area for basking. It will also need a cooler area in the centre of the tank where it can be active, while the far end of the tank should be even cooler still so your snake can cool down. Use a thermometer to check the temperature in the different parts of the tank. If the temperature drops lower than 23 °Celsius (74 °Fahrenheit) in any part of the tank, your snake might not want to eat and could get sick.

SAFETY FIRST

Never use a "hot rock" (a heater that looks like a rock) as a heat source for your snake. It could get burnt!

Turn out the lights

Snakes like it to be dark for at least 12 hours a day. Make sure your heat source does not produce a lot of light and remember to turn off lights at night so your snake can sleep!

WHICH HEAT SOURCE?

There are several ways to heat your snake's home.

✪ You could use a light bulb that produces a lot of heat. You must carefully monitor the temperature in the tank until you have found the correct wattage needed to provide the proper temperature for your snake. A light bulb should not be placed inside the tank because the snake might get burnt.

✪ A ceramic bulb produces heat but no light and its temperature can be adjusted. A ceramic bulb must not be kept in the tank as it can cause burns.

✪ You may choose to use heating pads or heating tape. These can be put under the tank to heat it from the bottom.

Ask a reptile **breeder** for advice on which would be the best heat source for you. Whichever type you choose, always make sure that your snake does not have direct access to the heat sources you use.

The temperature at the heated end of the tank (pictured) should be around 32°C (90°F). The temperature in the middle of the tank should be around 26°C (79°F), while the temperature at the far end should be about 24°C (75°F).

Feeding your snake

All snakes are **carnivorous**, which means that they eat other live animals. Both corn snakes and garter snakes eat a variety of live animals in the wild. When they are young they eat some insects, frogs, small lizards, **rodents**, and even eggs!

Dinnertime

Snakes are fun to feed! Since corn snakes are mainly **nocturnal** (more active at night), it is a good idea to feed them either late in the evening or early in the morning. You will enjoy watching your corn snake or garter snake smell, grab, and swallow its food – it is a fascinating sight!

Some snakes can stretch their jaws wide enough to swallow surprisingly large objects.

Young snakes enjoy eating crickets. You can buy containers of crickets like these from a pet shop or reptile breeder.

If your snake is young when you get it, you can offer it crickets and very small frozen mice. You can get these from a pet shop or a **reptile breeder**. The frozen **prey** will have to be defrosted first. Talk to an adult about the best way to defrost these animals. Snakes normally eat warm, live animals so you may want to warm them up by soaking them in warm water. Do *not* use a microwave to defrost frozen prey. It will become cooked and will not be very good for your snake.

TOP TIP

It is best not to feed your snake with live mice. If your snake does not eat the animals as soon as they are offered, they might bite your pet and injure it severely. Also, just think how frightening it is for a live mouse to be stuck in a tank with a snake! It is actually **illegal** in some countries to feed live prey to snakes!

Growing well?

A baby snake should grow pretty fast. If it is **shedding** its skin every three to four weeks, it is probably growing at a good pace. It is a good idea to measure and weigh your snake every week or so. You will need a simple weighing scale and a measuring tape.

Buy a scale to use only for weighing your snake. Never use your kitchen scale to weigh your snake, as snakes can leave behind **bacteria** that are dangerous to people. Try to weigh and measure your young snake regularly to make sure it is growing steadily.

HOW OFTEN? HOW MUCH?

Snakes take a very long time to digest their food so they do not need to be fed very often.

- ✪ Very young corn snakes should be offered food every 5 to 7 days. They can be fed one small newborn mouse or several crickets.

- ✪ **Juvenile** corn snakes (snakes that are less than 1 year old) can be fed every 7 to 10 days. One large mouse is about right.

- ✪ Adult corn snakes should be fed once every 10 to 14 days. They will eat two large mice or one medium rat at each mealtime.

Check with a reptile keeper or pet shop owner to see how much you should feed your snake. As your snake grows, it may eat less and not as often.

Encouraging your snake

Your snake will probably eat the food you give it. But you might need to encourage it a bit. Ask an adult to help you open up the mouse or rat so your snake can smell it better. You could also try using tongs or something similar to make the prey "move" a little in the tank. Your snake might think it is alive and be more likely to eat it!

TOP TIP

Do not use your fingers to hold the prey as you move it. Your snake might not be able to tell the difference between the prey and your fingers, and could bite you! Always wash your hands with soap and water after handling your snake's prey.

Sometimes you can persuade your snake that its food is alive by holding it with tongs and moving it around.

A little variety

Feeding pre-frozen rodents to your snake will provide it with a balanced, **nutritious** meal, but your snake will appreciate some variety. Other things that can be occasionally fed to your snake include frozen chicks and quail eggs. However, these do not include all the nutrients your snake needs. The chicks should be one to two days old. Your snake will eat two or three quail eggs at a time.

Big bulge?

After your snake has swallowed its prey, you might notice a bulge in its body. This bulge should not be too big. If it is very large, your snake might be having trouble digesting its food. Next time, feed your snake smaller prey.

TOP TIP

It will take several days for your snake to digest its food. To digest their food well, snakes need to be warm and quiet. Do not handle your snake for at least two days after you have fed it. It needs to rest to digest!

This snake has just eaten a meal. Can you see the bulge in its body?

Handling your snake

Snakes may look slimy and hard, but actually they are very soft and dry! Snakes are wonderful to touch and hold, but imagine how big you must seem to a young snake.

Do not be surprised if when you try to pick up your snake the first few times, it seems frightened and tries to slither away. This is normal. In the wild, a snake has lots of enemies – mostly larger animals and birds trying to eat it. Its main defence is to slither away as fast as it can and hide.

SLOWLY DOES IT

✪ It is best to let your snake get used to the idea of having your hand in its tank before you try to touch it. Move your hand around very gently until your snake realizes that your hand is not going to hurt it.

✪ When your snake is used to your hand in its tank, you can slowly start to touch your pet. First try just stroking your snake with one finger. When it seems used to that, try picking it up slowly.

When you put your hand in the tank, don't make loud noises. Move slowly. With a little patience, you can train your snake to get used to your hand in the tank. Then, slowly you can touch it.

Picking up your snake

The best way to pick up a snake is to scoop it up gently. Use one hand to hold it gently behind the head and the other hand to support the rest of its body. *Never* hold your snake with just one hand. It is best to hold your snake over a surface, like a bed or table, in case it wriggles free!

SNAKE-PROOFING YOUR ROOM

Before you pick up your snake, take a good look around. If your pet gets away while you are holding it, where will it go? Spend a few minutes "snake-proofing" your room before you take it out of the tank.

✪ Remove any sharp objects that could injure your snake.

✪ Make sure there are no holes or spaces that your snake could slip into and then be impossible to find or rescue!

✪ Do not handle your snake for more than 10 to 15 minutes. After this length of time, the snake should be returned to its tank.

Your snake will feel much more secure if you hold it close to your body. You will also be less likely to drop it!

Snakes are curious

Snakes are very curious, so your pet's first instinct will be to crawl in and out of your fingers, around your arms, and maybe even inside your shirt sleeves! It is quite surprising to feel the muscles of the snake moving on your arm!

Escape artist!

If your snake tries to get away, gently pick it up by its body and bring it back to your hands. But if your snake is constantly trying to get away, it is time to put it back in its tank! It is probably still a little nervous of being touched and needs a rest in order to calm down.

It might feel a little strange to have a snake inside your shirt, but do not worry – it will not hurt you!

GETTING TO KNOW YOU

You might also notice that your snake is flicking its tongue a lot when you hold it. This is its way of smelling you and recognizing you! If you handle your snake regularly, it will get used to you. After a few weeks, it will calmly sit on your hands.

If your snake bites...

If your snake is not used to you or if something frightens it, it might get scared and bite you. Do not panic! Corn snakes and garter snakes are unlikely to hurt you because their teeth are very small. If your snake does bite you, you might sometimes find it does not want to let go straight away. That is normal. Do not try to pull its mouth away from your hand, but support the snake with your other hand and tell an adult straight away. Once your snake has let go, wash your tiny cuts thoroughly and apply some antiseptic ointment. Your parents or guardians may take you to a doctor.

Do not worry if your snake flicks its tongue out a lot – it is just getting to know your scent!

Snake teeth can come out when the snake bites its **prey**, or you. Do not worry about this, your snake will grow some new teeth soon.

SAFETY FIRST

Even a healthy, clean snake can have **bacteria** on its body that could make you sick. To avoid any danger of spreading bacteria, follow these simple rules:

- ✪ Wash your hands with warm water and soap every time you finish handling your snake.
- ✪ Do not eat or drink while you are playing with your snake.
- ✪ Do not let your snake slither across places where you put food, such as kitchen worktops.

Some health problems

Whenever you take your snake out of its tank, check it carefully. It should have a filled-out, rounded body without any wrinkles and it should look **alert** and active. If your snake is slow and sluggish it may just be too cold. Check your thermometer to make sure that the tank is warm enough.

If you are not sure how to read a thermometer, ask an adult to help you. It is important to get it right.

Corn snakes and garter snakes are usually healthy, but they sometimes develop a few health problems. The next few pages describe some problems that your pet might experience.

When snakes get too cold they become very still and take less interest in their surroundings.

Not drinking

Most **reptiles** can survive for days or even weeks without food, but they cannot survive without water. Make sure your snake has clean, fresh water every day. If your snake is not drinking, contact the vet for advice.

Not eating

There are many reasons why your snake might not eat. It might be too cold, or too ill, or it might not like the food you are offering it. Sometimes snakes get tired of eating the same thing all the time. Try a different food and see if your pet starts to eat again.

If your snake is still not eating, even after you have changed its diet, look at it carefully for signs such as wrinkled skin or slow movement. If you are worried, ask an adult for their opinion. You may need to take it to the vet.

If your snake shows any signs of illness, contact your vet. You may need to take your pet for a check-up.

Shedding problems

If you notice that your snake is not **shedding** its skin well – if parts of its old skin are stuck to it or it is not shedding in one piece – then it might need some help. Place a bowl of warm water in the tank. The bowl should be large enough for your snake to get into, and contain enough warm water to cover the snake. Never try to rub off skin that has not been shed. If there is still skin hanging onto parts of your snake's body once it has soaked in its bath, talk to an adult about taking your snake to the vet.

Sometimes a warm bath can help your snake to finish shedding normally. You can see that this snake is shedding because its eyes are covered with old blue, or milky-looking, skin.

Vomiting

If you find that your snake is vomiting the food you feed it, you might be feeding it too much at once. Next time, give it less, or feed it two smaller animals instead of one large one. Another cause of vomiting is handling your snake too soon after it has eaten. If the problem continues, tell an adult.

DANGER SIGNS

Look out for the following warning signs. They could mean that your snake is seriously ill.

✪ Is your snake not interested in food, even after you have changed its diet?

✪ Does your snake seem less active than usual, even when the temperature in its tank is warm enough?

✪ Does it not respond to your hand or touch like it used to?

✪ Does its skin look saggy and wrinkly?

✪ Does it look skinny?

✪ Does it have any lumps or bumps on its skin?

✪ Has part or all of your snake's skin turned a different colour?

Checking your snake regularly is the best way to make sure that any problems are spotted as early as possible.

Visiting the vet

Just as you went to a doctor for check-ups when you were a baby, your snake will also need to visit a vet for a physical examination. Soon after you buy your snake, ask an adult to make an appointment with a vet who is used to working with reptiles. This will give your vet a chance to meet your snake. The vet will also be able to give you useful advice on how to care for your pet and how to recognize when it might be ill.

Soon after you get your pet, take it to the vet for a check-up.

CHECKING YOUR PET

Your vet will want to give your snake a thorough physical examination. During the examination the vet will probably:

- ✪ weigh your snake
- ✪ watch your snake to make sure it is active and lively
- ✪ look for **mites** and other skin **parasites**
- ✪ make sure the snake is not too skinny
- ✪ open the snake's mouth and look at its teeth and gums
- ✪ feel the snake's body to make sure its **organs** are normal
- ✪ listen to its heart and lungs
- ✪ check a sample of your snake's **faeces** to make sure they do not contain parasites.

The vet will give your snake a thorough physical examination.

Saying goodbye

Corn snakes and garter snakes can live as long as 10 to 15 years, but however well you care for your pet, one day it will die. Sometimes a snake will die unexpectedly. This will come as a shock to you, but do not blame yourself. There is probably nothing you could have done.

As a caring owner, it is hard to know when to let your pet be **put down** to save it from suffering. Your snake may be very old and in pain or it may have a serious illness. Your vet will give your snake a small injection. This does not hurt your pet. It will simply make your snake sleepy and its heart will stop beating.

FEELING UPSET

You will feel upset when your snake dies, especially if it has been a friend for many years. It is perfectly normal for people to be sad when a pet dies. It can help to have a special burial place and plant a flower or a shrub on it. Eventually, the pain will pass and you will be left with happy memories of your pet.

Keeping a record

It is fun to keep a record of your pet snake. Buy a big scrapbook and fill it with notes and photos. Then you can look back at it and remind yourself of all the things you and your pet have done together. Your snake scrapbook can also include general information about snakes and how to care for them.

Pictures

Take pictures of your snake every few months and put them in your snake scrapbook. It will be fascinating to look back later and see how your snake has grown.

You will soon build up a very useful record of your pet, but remember to put the fun things in too!

A SPECIAL SCRAPBOOK

There are many things you can write in your scrapbook.

✪ Describe your trip to the pet shop or reptile breeder to buy your snake. What did your snake look like and how did you feel about it?

✪ Write down the name you chose for your pet.

✪ Note down special events in the life of your snake, such as the first time it shed its skin.

✪ Make a note of all the cool things your snake does, such as winding its way inside your shirt!

Important information

Your scrapbook is a very good place to keep important information. Write down the phone number of your vet, your local **reptile breeder**, and the company where you buy your snake's food. Because you do not need to feed your snake very often, it is a good idea to note down when you last fed your snake and how much it ate. It is also helpful to keep a record of your snake's weight each time you weigh it. That way you can see if it is growing steadily. Similarly, write down when your snake **sheds** its skin so you can make sure that it is shedding regularly.

Black rat snake

Corn snake

Add labels to the pictures after you have stuck them in. Otherwise you might forget what they are!

TOP TIP

You can cut out articles and pictures of snakes from magazines and stick them in your scrapbook.

Understanding snakes

Snakes have often had a negative image. False beliefs caused people to fear snakes. Some people still wrongly believe that all snakes bite people and are poisonous. People have killed snakes with poison, in traps, or by beating them to death. Many of these snake deaths come from people's **ignorance** and fear.

But if snakes are eliminated from the areas that their **rodent prey** inhabit, the prey multiplies and often causes the spread of diseases or the destruction of property. It is important that we recognize the good snakes do, and help others understand how they help keep our ecosystem in balance.

SHARING THE FUN

There are many people who love snakes as much as you do! Ask a **reptile breeder** or at your pet shop if they know of a snake club in your local area that you could join. Getting together with other people who appreciate snakes can be fun. They can tell you about their experiences and you can share your stories too.

It is fun to meet other snake owners and share useful tips about looking after your pets.

NOW TRY THIS

Here are some more ways to find out about snakes:

✪ Visit your local library and bookshop – there are hundreds of books written on snakes.

✪ Go to zoos and nature centres – they will have amazing snakes to see and lots of information on snakes in the wild.

✪ With an adult, visit other snake lovers' websites and the websites of reptile breeders. You will see beautiful pictures of many types of snake and read about their unusual lives.

✪ Go to a magazine shop and find out what magazines they have on snakes or reptiles. A good magazine will contain lots of useful information.

Most zoos have a reptile house with a wide range of interesting snakes – some of the snakes in zoos are incredibly dangerous!

Glossary

albino animal or person with very light or white skin, fur, or hair

alert always watchful and paying attention

bacteria tiny one-celled creatures that can cause disease

bask to lie in the sun and absorb its warmth

breed mate and produce young

breeder someone who keeps animals and encourages them to mate and produce young

camouflage colours and markings to help blend in with surroundings

captivity under the control of humans

carnivorous meat-eating

cold-blooded animal having the same body temperature as the surrounding air or water

constriction coiling around prey in order to strangle it

deforestation cutting down forests in order to use the wood or to clear the land for farming or construction

endangered at risk of being completely wiped out

environment surroundings and weather conditions in an area

faeces solid waste matter (poo) passed out of the body, also called droppings

fang long, pointed tooth

habitat place where an animal or plant lives or grows

heat source place where warmth or heat comes from, such as the Sun

ignorance lack of knowledge

illegal against the law

juvenile young or immature animal

mite small blood-sucking insect

nocturnal animal that is active at night

nutritious food source that provides the energy needed by an animal

organ part of the body that has a specific purpose

parasite small creature, such as a tick or worm, that lives on or in another animal

particle very small piece of something

pesticide substance that kills insects or other pests that are harmful to plants

poultry farm birds, such as chickens, turkeys, ducks, or geese

predator animal that lives by killing and eating other animals

prey animal killed by another animal for food

put down give a sick animal an injection to help it die peacefully and without pain

reptile cold-blooded animal with scaly or tough skin

rodent member of the animal family that includes rats, mice, and voles

scent gland special place on some animals where they produce a smelly substance that can be spread around to mark their territory

shed lose a covering, such as a snake shedding its skin

species group of animals that is similar and can produce young

substrate soft material put in the bottom of a snake tank

suffocate stop breathing. This leads to death.

tick small creature that lives on another animal's skin and sucks its blood

venom poison made by some animals to inject into their enemies or prey

venom gland place on an animal where the venom is produced

venomous animal that attacks its prey or enemies using venom

Find out more

Books

There are not many books about snakes written for young readers, but the ones below can be enjoyed by snake owners of all ages.

Corn and Rat Snakes, Philip Purser (TFH Publications, 2006)

Corn Snakes and Other Rat Snakes, Richard and Patricia Bartlett (Barron's Educational Series, 2006)

Corn Snakes: The Comprehensive Owner's Guide, Kathy and Bill Love (Advanced Vivarium Systems Inc., 2005)

Snakes!, Melissa Stewart (National Geographic Society, 2009)

Websites

www.thecornsnake.co.uk
This website has lots of photos, information, and helpful advice on keeping corn snakes as pets.

www.thebhs.org
This website has information on the British Herpetological Society and the Young Herpetologists' Club.

www.britishzoos.co.uk
This website provides details on zoos in the United Kingdom, which you might want to visit to learn more about snakes and other reptiles.

Index